CORTÉS

Great Explorers of the World

Conquering the Powerful Aztec Empire

Carl R. Green

Enslow Publishers, Inc.
40 Industrial Road
Box 398
Berkeley Heights, NJ 07922
USA

http://www.enslow.com

This book is dedicated to my loving and patient wife,
who gives me the time and space I need
for my research and writing.

Library of Congress Cataloging-in-Publication Data

Green, Carl R.
  Cortés : conquering the powerful Aztec empire / Carl R. Green.
    p. cm. — (Great explorers of the world)
  Includes bibliographical references and index.
  Summary: "Examines the life of Spanish conquistador Hernán Cortés, including his first voyages to
the New World, his conquering of the Aztec Empire, and his legacy in world history"—Provided by
publisher.
  ISBN-13: 978-1-59845-099-6
  ISBN-10: 1-59845-099-9
  1. Cortés, Hernán, 1485–1547—Juvenile literature. 2. Mexico—History—Conquest,
1519–1540—Juvenile literature. 3. Montezuma II, Emperor of Mexico, ca. 1480–1520—Juvenile
literature. 4. Aztecs—History—Juvenile literature. I. Title.
  F1230.C835G74 2010
  972'.02092—dc22

                                    2009021377

Printed in the United States of America

102009 Lake Book Manufacturing, Inc., Melrose Park, IL

10 9 8 7 6 5 4 3 2 1

To Our Readers:
We have done our best to make sure all Internet Addresses in this book were active and appropriate
when we went to press. However, the author and the publisher have no control over and assume no
liability for the material available on those Internet sites or on other Web sites they may link to. Any
comments or suggestions can be sent by e-mail to comments@enslow.com or to the address on the
back cover.

✪ Enslow Publishers, Inc., is committed to printing our books on recycled paper. The paper in every
book contains 10% to 30% post-consumer waste (PCW). The cover board on the outside of each book
contains 100% PCW. Our goal is to do our part to help young people and the environment too!

Illustration Credits: © AISA / Everett Collection, pp. 15, 92; The Art Archive / Private Collection / Eileen
Tweedy, p. 31; Associated Press, pp. 56–57, 84; Enslow Publishers, Inc., p. 66; Erich Lessing / Art Resource, NY,
p. 26; The Granger Collection, New York, pp. 13, 37, 63, 79; © 2009 Jupiterimages Corporation, pp. 1, 42, 48,
72, 77, 96; Keystone / Eyedea / Everett Collection, p. 50; Library of Congress, pp. 17, 46, 55; Mary Evans Picture
Library / Edwin Wallace / Everett Collection, p. 59; © Mel Longhurst / Impact / HIP / The Image Works, pp. 9,
38–39; Vanni / Art Resource, NY, pp. 20–21.

Ship Illustration Used in Chapter Openers: © 2009 Jupiterimages Corporation.

Cover Illustration: © 2009 Jupiterimages Corporation (Portrait of Hernán Cortés).

Contents

EXPLORER TIMELINE

1325— Aztecs found their capital city of Tenochtitlán in the Valley of Mexico.

1485— Hernán Cortés is born in Medellín in Spain's province of Extremadura.

1499— Cortés begins studying law at the University of Salamanca, but drops out two years later.

1504— Eager to win fame and fortune, Cortés books passage to Hispaniola. He is given a land grant and thrives as a farmer.

1511— Diego Velázquez, with Cortés as his supply officer, leads the invasion of Cuba.

1511 –1518 Cortés prospers as a landowner, but he falls in and out of favor with Velázquez. The governor picks him to lead an expedition to Yucatán.

1519— *March:* Cortés lands in Mexico. He enlists Indian allies and encounters Malinche, who becomes his interpreter.

July: Cortés marches toward the Aztec capital after disabling his ships.

November: The expedition enters Tenochtitlán and Cortés meets Montezuma. Six days later he makes the emperor his prisoner.

1520— *May:* Cortés returns to the coast and defeats a force sent by Velázquez to arrest him.

June: Montezuma is killed during a bloody Aztec uprising.

July 1: The Spanish suffer heavy casualties as they flee Tenochtitlán on *La Noche Triste*.

1521— *April to August:* Cortés and his Indian allies destroy the smallpox-ravaged Aztec capital.

1528— Cortés returns to Spain, where the king honors him with a title.

1530— Back in Mexico, Cortés settles on an estate in Cuernavaca.

1533— Cortés discovers Baja California and gives his
−1534　name to the Sea of Cortés.

1540— Cortés sails back to Spain, where government infighting strips him of his authority. His name is blackened by rumors that he murdered his wife.

1547— *December 2:* The ailing sixty-three-year-old conquistador dies in Seville.

1810— Mexico fights for and wins its independence
−1823　from Spain.

1824— Mexico becomes a federal republic.

1846— The United States defeats Mexico and annexes
−1848　the American Southwest.

Chapter 1

A Conquistador Comes of Age

The dawn of the 1500s found western Europe bursting with excitement. From the kings and dukes to the shopkeepers and peasants, people sensed that change was in the air. The new age had begun in 1492, when Christopher Columbus planted the Spanish flag in the New World. Spanish colonies were taking root in the fertile soil of the West Indies. Young men sharpened their swords and dreamed of winning fame and fortune in far-off lands.

In 1504, one of those teenagers arrived on Hispaniola (the present-day island divided between Haiti and the Dominican Republic). Hernán Cortés was determined, brave, and well schooled. Because the island needed colonists, the governor's secretary offered the newcomer a very generous land grant. In return, Cortés agreed to work his *encomienda* for at least five years. He also promised to convert the Taino Indians who lived there. In return, he was allowed to put the Taino to work in his fields.

To a restless nineteen-year-old, five years must have sounded like a life sentence. Legend says that Cortés told the governor's secretary, "Neither in this island nor in any other part of the New World do I wish . . . to stay so long."[1]

Even so, Cortés kept his end of the bargain. He raised sugarcane and cassava (a starchy root crop) with the help of his Taino workers. In his spare time, he hunted wild game and searched vainly for gold. When called on to join expeditions sent to fend off Indian rebels, he fought bravely and well. Cortés also earned respect by serving as a public notary (a recorder of events).

The years slipped past. Still eager for gold and glory, Cortés told friends that it was time to spin the wheel of fortune. He would "either dine to the sound of trumpets," he said, "or die on the scaffold."[2]

A New Conquest

In pursuit of his goal, Cortés sought the favor of the rich and powerful. Governor Diego Velázquez responded by taking Cortés under his wing. When he asked the young man to join the force he was raising to invade Cuba, Cortés jumped at the chance. Late in 1511, the expedition set sail for Cuba with Cortés as its supply officer.

The well-armed invaders easily subdued the local Taino Indians. As the campaign progressed, Cortés emerged as one of the governor's most trusted aides. Fearless and handy with a sword, he also earned the respect of his fellow soldiers. One

This is a reproduction of a Taino village in Chorro de Maita, Cuba. Cortés had Taino Indians working on his farm in Hispaniola and he fought against them when he subdued a rebellion in Cuba.

report says that he "behaved so bravely . . . that in a short time he became the most experienced man of all."[3]

Once they had overrun the island, the Spanish turned to the hard work of settlement. As with any new colony, there were fields to plow and towns to build. Cortés, with Velázquez as his patron, threw himself into this new challenge. Awarded a fine *encomienda,* he built a house, planted crops, and raised cattle and horses. His future looked even brighter when he found placer gold in the local streams.[4]

CHIEF HATUEY TELLS THE SPANISH WHAT HE THINKS OF THEM

Cuba fell quickly to Velázquez and his men. Except for a chief named Hatuey and his followers, the local Taino offered little resistance. When the Spanish captured the fierce chief, Velázquez sentenced him to be burned at the stake. While the soldiers gathered wood for the fire, a Catholic friar approached Hatuey. "Give your heart to God," the holy man told him. "As a Christian, you will earn a quick death by the sword and a place in heaven."

Hatuey, the story goes, asked if there would be Spaniards in heaven. Told that they would be there in great numbers, the chief shook his head. "Then I will not be a Christian," he told the friar, "for I would not go again to a place where I must find men so cruel!"[5]

IN AND OUT OF FAVOR

Cortés's future should have been secure. He was growing wealthy and he had the governor's favor. All that changed with the arrival of the Juárez family. Juan Juárez, with his mother and sisters, had landed on Hispaniola in 1509. Spanish women were scarce in the Indies, and Catalina and Leonor, Juárez's two sisters, attracted a host of suitors. For a time, however, marriage eluded them. Their prospects improved when they moved to Cuba as ladies-in-waiting to Velázquez's bride-to-be. When the bride died soon after the wedding, Leonor took her place in the governor's heart.

Catalina plunged into a torrid romance with Cortés. Her lover, however, was in no hurry to marry. Catalina did her best to lead him to the altar, but Cortés eluded her. When word of their affair reached Velázquez, he was enraged. Cortés, the governor charged, was not playing fair with Leonor's sister. But before the dispute could be resolved, it was eclipsed by a more serious matter.

For quite some time, a secret group had been plotting to unseat the governor. Velázquez, the members charged, had saved the best land and jobs for his friends. In 1514, even though he had little cause to complain, Cortés joined the group. The members looked to him for leadership and often met at his home. Perhaps Cortés hoped to take Velázquez's place—or he simply may have enjoyed the thrill of hatching a scheme.[6]

LOCKED IN A PRISON CELL

The plot collapsed just as Cortés was about to carry the group's petition to Hispaniola. Velázquez, tipped off by his spies, locked his friend in a cell in Santiago de Cuba. The governor could have sent Cortés to the gallows, but he hesitated. The delay gave Cortés a chance to escape and take refuge in a nearby church. Thanks to the customs of the day, he was safe there as long as he did not leave.[7]

The days Cortés spent in the church must have seemed endless. One day, bored and restless, he slipped out to greet Catalina as she entered the churchyard. Moments later, watchful guards were dragging him back to prison. An angry Velázquez told the soldiers to bind Cortés with chains and ship him to Hispaniola for trial. Thrown into the hold of a ship, Cortés somehow slipped his chains and stole a small boat. As he rowed toward shore, a strong tide threatened to sweep him out to sea. Cortés saved himself by swimming to shore.[8]

Holed up again in the church, Cortés met with Juan Juárez. He was ready, he claimed, to marry Catalina. His change of heart was well timed, for Velázquez needed help in putting down a Taino uprising. Once the Indian threat ended, Cortés moved Catalina into a fine home and showered her with gifts. For a time, he even served as *alcalde* (mayor) of Santiago.

A NEW ADVENTURE— AND NEW CONFLICTS

In 1517, an expedition led by Francisco de Córdoba landed at Cape Catoche on the Yucatán Peninsula. There, the Spaniards met the warlike Maya Indians for the first time. The invaders won the first clashes, thanks to their armor and firepower. They also caught their first glimpse of the Maya's splendid temples. The thrill of discovery soon faded, however. Fifty soldiers died when warriors ambushed the column. Córdoba, badly

This Mayan mask crafted from a thin sheet of gold was found in Yucatán, Mexico. In 1517, the small bag of Mayan gold that Francisco de Córdoba brought back from his journey spurred Governor Diego Velázquez to send more explorers to Mexico.

wounded, ordered his men back to their ships. Bloodied and weary, the tiny fleet had to limp home to Cuba.[9]

Córdoba's report—plus a small bag of Mayan gold—inspired visions of rich new colonies. In May 1518, Velázquez dispatched his nephew, Juan de Grijalva, with a second fleet. Like Córdoba, Grijalva met strong resistance in Yucatán. Rather than risk further bloodshed, he rounded the peninsula and crossed the Gulf of Campeche. When he landed at Tabasco, he found the local Totonac Indians very eager to trade. The Totonac happily exchanged fine cloaks and gold jewelry for glass beads, mirrors, and bits of clothing. The Spaniards marveled at the region's stone cities—and tales of a far richer culture to the west.[10]

Velázquez was overjoyed when the first of Grijalva's ships returned to Cuba. Pedro de Alvarado delivered his captain's report—and about twenty thousand pesos worth of gold. Anxious to beat his bosses on Hispaniola to this new land, Velázquez planned a third expedition. Rather than spend his own money, he looked for someone else to pay the bulk of the costs. Urged on by Cortés's friends, Velázquez offered the task to the young soldier. Cortés jumped at the chance.[11]

The expedition quickly took shape under the new captain-general's prodding. Soldiers, many of whom had sailed with Córdoba and Grijalva, flocked to his banner. Cortés also gathered stocks of food and weapons. When he ran short of cash, he borrowed from his wealthy friends. He also recruited two hundred Taino to serve as porters, cooks, and servants.

For transport, Cortés rounded up a fleet of eleven ships. As the days raced past, workmen packed the ships with live pigs and turkeys, salted meats, maize, wine, oil, and sugar. Along with the soldiers' armor, porters loaded swords, lances, javelins, and crossbows. For firearms, Cortés had to make do with thirteen muskets, ten brass guns,

Velázquez entrusted Cortés with the mission to explore the newly discovered land of Mexico. In this painting, the two men discuss the upcoming expedition.

"Let Us Follow the Sign of the Holy Cross"

At age seventy, Bernal Díaz del Castillo sat down to write his "true and wonderful" *History of the Conquest of New Spain*. The aging conquistador knew the story well, for he had shared that epic adventure with Hernán Cortés. In an early chapter, Díaz describes the captain-general's preparations for his mission:

> As soon as Hernando Cortés was appointed General, he began to collect arms of all kinds—guns, powder, and crossbows—and all the munitions of war he could find. . . . Moreover, he began to adorn himself and to take much more care of his appearance than before. He wore a plume of feathers, with a medallion and a gold chain, and a velvet cloak trimmed with loops of gold. . . . He then had two standards and banners made, worked in gold with the royal arms and a cross on each side and a legend that read: "Brothers and comrades, let us follow the sign of the Holy Cross in true faith, for under this sign we shall conquer."[12]

and four small cannons. He also found room for a pack of dogs and sixteen horses. The horses were costly, but Cortés had a hunch that they would more than pay for themselves.[13]

All seemed well until a rival group caught the governor's ear. Cortés, they warned, could not be trusted. To calm those fears, Cortés assured Velázquez over and over that he would make them both rich. Then, on November 18, 1518, Cortés abruptly ordered his men to board their ships.

Velázquez viewed this sudden move as proof that his friends were right. He rushed to the harbor, ready to relieve Cortés of his command. The governor reached the quay just as Cortés stepped into a small boat.

"And is it thus you part from me!" shouted Velázquez.

"Pardon me!" Cortés shouted back. "Time presses, and there are some things that should be done. . . . Has your Excellency any commands?"

Taken aback, Velázquez fell silent. Cortés waved good-bye and ordered his sailors to take up their oars. Minutes later, he boarded his flagship and led the small fleet out to sea.[14]

Hernán Cortés takes his leave of Cuba as Governor Velázquez angrily shouts at him from the shore.

Chapter 2

A New World Calls

Diego Velázquez was one of Spain's better colonial governors. Accustomed to having his orders obeyed, he never dreamed that Cortés would defy him. His new captain-general, he later learned, had been surprising people all his life.

A Sickly Child Grows to Robust Manhood

Hernán Cortés was born in 1485 in the Spanish city of Medellín. The city lay in the remote western province of Extremadura. It was a bleak, windswept land, a region known for turning out hard and ambitious men. During the 1500s, some of those men found fame in the New World. Along with Cortés, their ranks included Vasco Nuñez de Balboa, Francisco Pizarro, and Hernando de Soto.[1]

The boy's parents, Martín Cortés de Monroy and his wife, Catalina, were far from wealthy. The soldier father must have despaired when he first saw his sickly son. Catalina, in keeping with custom, handed Hernán to a wet nurse. The woman breast-fed the baby and prayed to

Hernán Cortés was born in the Spanish city of Medellín. This statue of Cortés stands in the city today.

St. Peter to spare his life. To her delight, the child survived and grew strong.[2]

Hernán learned to ride horses at an early age. With his friends, he spent long hours practicing the arts of war in an old castle. On Sundays and feast days, Hernán served as an altar boy at his local church. Those duties left him with a strong faith in the Catholic Church and its teachings.[3]

● THE LONG, HARD ROAD TO THE INDIES

Hernán's parents set their son on the career path they had chosen when he was fourteen. Given his quick mind, they judged, the boy would make a good lawyer. As a first step, they sent him north to Salamanca to study Latin and grammar. In his free time, Cortés read widely and indulged a newfound passion for gambling.[4]

Two years later, in 1501, Cortés dropped out of school. The quiet life of a lawyer did not suit his restless spirit. The fame he craved, he thought, could best be found on the battlefield. With his parents' reluctant blessing, he decided to join an expedition to the New World. It was led by Nicolás de Ovando, a family friend and Hispaniola's new governor.[5]

Cortés drifted in and out of love affairs while he waited for the fleet to sail. A late night visit to a young wife, however, nearly cost Cortés his life.

As he climbed out of her window, a wall collapsed under his weight. The crash awoke the woman's husband, who grabbed his sword and rushed to the scene. If the girl's mother had not pulled him away, the angry husband would likely have killed the helpless Cortés.[6]

With Cortés hobbled by injuries, Ovando sailed without him. After Cortés recovered, the teenager spent a year wandering through the Spanish cities of Seville, Valencia, and Granada. By the time he returned to Medellín, he was again focused on the Indies. Anxious to see their son make a name for himself, his parents paid for his passage.[7]

WHAT KIND OF MAN WAS THE GREAT CONQUISTADOR?

By modern standards, Hernán Cortés did not look like a great hero. Historian Hugh Thomas describes him as standing five feet, four inches tall (slightly above average for the 1500s). He had "a deep chest, no belly to speak of and was bow-legged." People who knew him described his hair as "fair," or "somewhat red."[8]

Historian William Prescott writes that Cortés was pale and viewed the world through large, dark eyes. Strong and agile, the captain-general was a skilled horseman who never flinched when facing danger. His soldiers, Prescott adds, obeyed his orders without question.[9] When they describe Cortés's character, other writers use words such as "lucky," "clever," "bold," and "ruthless."[10]

ELUDING VELÁZQUEZ'S NET

When Cortés finally reached Hispaniola, the clever nineteen-year-old caught Diego Velázquez's eye. The friendship took Cortés to Cuba and a leading role in the new colony. The two men were often at odds, but the governor relaxed his guard after Cortés married Catalina Juaréz. When Velázquez needed someone to lead an expedition to Yucatán, he turned to Cortés. All seemed well—until the fateful day that the governor changed his mind.

After Cortés left the governor fuming on the dock, Velázquez played his next card. Knowing that the fleet would stop at Trinidad on Cuba's south coast, he ordered the mayor to arrest the bold captain-general. Mayor Verdugo, however, wilted when he met Cortés. Instead of jailing him, Verdugo ignored the order. He also helped Cortés round up more horses and supplies.[11]

A similar drama took place at Havana, Cuba, where local officials jumped to do Cortés's bidding. Few could blame them, for the expedition's well-armed soldiers were fiercely protective of their leader. Cortés had won their hearts with a stirring speech.[12]

COZUMEL: FIRST CONTACT

On February 18, 1519, the expedition sailed west. By this time, Cortés had enlisted some five hundred tough fighting men. Along with supplies and

CORTÉS WINS THE TRUST OF HIS MEN

Cortés gave his men a stirring pep talk before the expedition left Cuba. His eloquent speech appealed to their love of country, their religious zeal, and their greed. "I hold out to you a glorious prize," he said, "but it is to be won by incessant toil. . . . Glory," he went on, "was never the reward of sloth. Be true to me, those of you who hope for riches. . . . I will make you masters of such as our countrymen have never dreamed of!"

By this time those "rough and turbulent" men were hanging on his every word. "You are few in number, but strong in resolution," Cortés told them. "If this does not falter, doubt not but that the Almighty . . . will shield you. . . . Go forward, then," he said, "and carry to a glorious issue the work so [well] begun."[13]

During Mass, a priest called on St. Peter to protect the expedition. Only then did the ships weigh anchor.

arms, the ships carried a jumble of trade goods. The Spanish hoped to exchange cheap bells, mirrors, beads, pins, and ribbons for Indian gold.[14]

A storm scattered the fleet as it steered a course toward Yucatán. When the skies cleared, the ships met near the island of Cozumel. Cortés, who had stopped to aid a damaged ship, arrived late. Pedro de Alvarado, one of his officers, had already landed. The sight of the bearded, light-skinned strangers sent the local Maya fleeing into the jungle. Alvarado and his men moved in and looted the deserted towns. When he saw the spoils, Cortés flew into a rage. The Indians, he cried, must be treated fairly.

Cortés landed in Mexico in 1519. This sixteenth-century illustration depicts his arrival in Mexico as the local Indians gather to greet him. Cortés is standing at center raising a flag.

He gave Alvarado a tongue-lashing and set out to repair the damage.[15]

To communicate, Cortés relied on an Indian who had been captured by an earlier expedition. Melchior, as the Indian had been baptized, spoke only a little Spanish. It was enough, however. Speaking through Melchior, Cortés told two of his prisoners to carry gifts to their *cacique* (chief). Lured by the presents, the Maya returned to their villages. Soon the Spanish were trading beads and mirrors for gold trinkets, fish, fruit, and honey.[16]

SMASHED IDOLS AND A NEW INTERPRETER

With peace restored, Cortés inspected his soldiers and their weapons. A check of his horses showed that the herd had grown. During the voyage one of the mares had given birth to a healthy colt.[17]

Cortés next set to work to convert the Maya to Christianity. When Melchior could not translate his religious message, the captain-general turned to a show of force. On Cortés's orders, soldiers climbed a pyramid and smashed its stone idols. Then they whitewashed the bloodstained stones and raised a wooden cross. As a final touch, the soldiers placed a carving of the Holy Mother on the altar. Awed by this new god's power, the islanders promised to honor him.[18]

Rumors soon reached the camp that Spaniards were living on the mainland. Cortés sent a crew to check out the story. When the sailors returned empty-handed, Cortés left Cozumel—but he came back almost at once. One of his ships was leaking and had to be beached for repairs. While the sailors patched the hull, some Indians landed a canoe nearby. As guards approached, swords ready, one of the boatmen spoke.

"*Señores*," the man said in broken Spanish, "are you Christians?"[19]

Taken to Cortés, the man said his name was Jerónimo de Aguilar. Born in Spain, he had trained for the priesthood. Dispatched to the New World to do missionary work, his ship had gone down near Yucatán. A boatload of survivors had reached the mainland, where they fell into Mayan hands. Only Aguilar and a sailor, Gonzalo Guerrero, had escaped being sacrificed.

Lost in the jungle, the men were captured by a powerful cacique. The chief, less cruel than most, decided to spare their lives. Guerrero married a Mayan woman and became a member of the tribe. True to his calling, Aguilar refused to marry. This angered the chief, who used him as a slave.[20] When Aguilar left to find Cortés, Guerrero stayed with his family. Because Aguilar could speak Mayan, Cortés now had a translator he could trust. Better still, Aguilar understood the Maya and their way of life.

🜨 FIRST BLOOD

On March 4, 1519, the Spanish ships left Cozumel and sailed down the west coast of Yucatán. A few days later, they dropped anchor at the mouth of the Tabasco River. Setting out in small boats, the Spaniards rowed upriver. Grijalva, they knew, had done some very fruitful trading there. The first Tabascan Indians they met, however, were armed and angry. Aguilar shouted that the Spanish had come in peace, but the warriors would not listen. Ever since they had traded with Grijalva, their neighboring villages had been laughing at them.

That night, the Tabascans hid their women and children and strengthened their stockade. Cortés, in turn, prepared for his first battle as captain-general. Under cover of darkness, he moved a hundred men into the woods behind the Tabascan village. At dawn, after hearing a priest say Mass, Cortés led the rest of his force upriver.

When he neared the village, Cortés told Aguilar to recite the *requerimiento*. As required by law, the translator told the Indians that they must bow to the rule of Christ and the king of Spain. If they refused, he warned, their future would be dark and bloody.[21] The Tabascans, very eager for battle, ignored the warning. His duty done, Cortés gave the order to attack. He lost a sandal as he splashed through thick mud, but he kept on going.

The warriors met the charging soldiers with a shower of darts and arrows. Protected by their shields, the soldiers broke through the stockade. As they surged into the village, the men hidden in the woods raced to join in the assault. In close combat, the Indians' stone-age weapons were no match for Spanish steel. After a few minutes of bloody fighting, the Tabascans broke and ran.

While his men cheered, Cortés cut three deep slashes in a silk-cotton tree. The symbolic act claimed the land "in the name of 'His Majesty the King.'"[22]

THE BATTLE OF CINTLA

For a few days, all seemed calm. Cortés sent his wounded soldiers back to the ships and unloaded the horses. A night in the grassy fields restored the spring to their step. Next, Cortés sent gifts of glass beads to the Tabascan caciques. The chiefs took the beads, but ignored Cortés's offer of peace. The reason soon became clear. Prisoners captured by Spanish scouts warned that thousands of warriors were gathering on the Plain of Cintla. Their plan was simple. First they would kill the invaders— then they would eat them.[23]

The two armies clashed on March 25, 1519. Hoping to surprise the Tabascan warriors, Cortés hid his cavalry in some nearby woods. By this time, his four hundred foot soldiers had engaged the huge Indian force. Bernal Díaz writes that the

Cortés and his soldiers battle the Tabascans. The two armies fought a bloody battle on the Plain of Cintla on March 25, 1519.

Indians were wearing "great feather crests, . . . their faces were painted black and white." They were armed, he says, with "bows and arrows, spears and shields, swords . . . and slings and stones and fire-toughened darts." The warriors "surrounded us, discharging such a rain of arrows, darts, and stones . . . that more than seventy of our men were wounded at the first attack."[24]

Spanish weapons and tactics saved the day. As the warriors rushed forward, the soldiers formed a tight square, their cannons stationed at the corners. Swinging their swords with deadly precision, the soldiers blunted the charge and forced the Indians

Chapter 3

A Battle of Wills: Cortés and Montezuma

With the gold stored away, Cortés told his captains to set sail for Mexico. Morale was high as the men prepared for the adventures that lay ahead.

A priest christened the Tabascan women that the Spanish men had received as a peace offering. Once they were Christians, Cortés said, the women would be free to serve the men's needs. In this group of short, plump women, one tall, beautiful young woman stood out. The priest christened her Marina, but history knows her as Malinche. This was a distortion of Malintzin, the name the Aztecs called her.[1]

TENDILE'S VISIT

The fleet left Tabasco on April 18. Sailing northwest, Cortés dropped anchor at an offshore island he called San Juan de Ulúa. Almost at once, a band of Totonac Indians paddled out to greet the white men. Aguilar was baffled when he tried to talk to them in Mayan. He learned later that they spoke Nahuatl, the language of the Aztecs.

Using signs, the Indians let Cortés know that they would return with their governor. To prepare for the visit, Cortés and his men landed on the mainland. Working quickly, the soldiers set up a fortified camp. As news of their arrival spread, Indians crowded in, eager to trade for beads, pins, and mirrors.[2]

On Easter Sunday, a line of Aztecs approached the camp. The nobles were dressed in fine feather cloaks and their servants carried gifts of food and gold. Tendile, the governor, greeted Cortés in the formal Aztec manner. Thanks to Aguilar and Malinche, Cortés was able to converse with him. The breakthrough had come when Aguilar learned that Nahuatl was Malinche's birth language. She soon mastered Spanish as well.[3]

Cortés told Tendile that he served a great and powerful king. His king, he said, wanted him to pay his respects to the governor's lord. Tendile promised to ask his emperor, Montezuma II, if a visit was in order. Next, hoping to impress their guests, the Spanish put on a show. Foot soldiers engaged in mock combat and the ground shook as horsemen galloped past. When the cannon roared, the startled Aztecs threw themselves to the ground. Cortés chose this particular moment to ask the shaken governor if Montezuma had any gold. When Tendile said that he did, Cortés had a ready response. "Send me some of it," he said. "I and my companions suffer from a disease of the heart which can be cured only with gold."[4]

MALINCHE: HEROINE OR TRAITOR?

Little is known about Malinche's early life. She likely was born around 1496, the daughter of an Aztec cacique. After her father died, her mother remarried and gave birth to a son. To clear the way for the boy to inherit, the mother sold Malinche to slave traders. After the Tabascans gave her to the Spanish in 1519, she seldom left Cortés's side.

Malinche's skills as a translator were priceless. Just as crucial was her ability to explain Indian thought and customs. As if to confirm her value, the Aztecs often addressed Cortés as "Malinche." Cortés did not object. One of his captains quoted him as saying that after God, Malinche was the key to his success.

Malinche gave birth to a son in 1522. Today, Mexico honors Martín Cortés as the first *mestizo* (child of mixed Indian and European blood). Malinche served again as an interpreter on Cortés's expedition to Honduras from 1524 to 1526. During that trip she married Juan Jaramillo, and bore him a daughter. Some accounts say she died in 1529; others argue that she might have lived until 1551.

In Mexico today, many people condemn Malinche as a traitor. A smaller group argues that without her, the conquest could have been far more destructive. The Aztec empire was destroyed, but the people and much of their culture survived.[5]

An Aztec drawing depicts Malinche (left) interpreting during a meeting between Cortés (seated) and the Aztec envoy who greeted him when he first landed on Aztec territory.

Tendile carried the message back to the Aztec capital, Tenochtitlán. When Tendile returned, his men carried a fresh supply of gifts. Along with a helmet filled with gold, Tendile gave Cortés two cartwheel-sized disks. The moon disk was made of silver, the sun disk of gold. Both were finely engraved with Aztec symbols.[6] Montezuma's reply to Cortés's request for a visit was less pleasing. A meeting, Tendile said, was out of the question.

Three Spanish cannons rest atop the El Morro Fortress in Old Havana, Cuba. The big guns are similar to the cannons that Cortés used to impress and frighten the Aztecs.

No Turning Back

The rich gifts further sharpened Cortés's hunger for conquest. He knew meeting the emperor would be a crucial step in that direction. For the moment, however, he was focused on another problem.

Cortés could not return to Cuba. If he did, Velázquez would arrest him and seize the gold. To solve that problem, Cortés urged his captains to set up a town council. Once they were sworn in, the councilmen created Villa Rica de Veracruz (the "rich town of the true cross"). The council then named Cortés the town's captain-general and chief justice. Thanks to his new status, Spanish law allowed him to report directly to the king.[7]

By this time, food was running short. Some Velázquez loyalists argued that it was time to head back to Cuba. Fearing a revolt, Cortés sentenced two of the men to be hanged. To cement his claim to royal favor, he then loaded a ship with Aztec gold and dispatched it to Spain. With the ship went a letter that begged King Charles to confirm Cortés in his new post. Next, pushing his luck to the limit, he announced that the ships' hulls were rotting. On his orders, the captains salvaged most of the equipment and supplies. Then they sank four of the ships and beached the other five. Without ships, no one could return to Cuba.[8]

As the expedition broke camp, Cortés assured the men that they were doing God's work. Heartened by his words, four hundred soldiers and a handful of horsemen followed him westward. Marching close behind was an army of Totonac warriors. After learning that the Totonac hated their Aztec masters, Cortés had promised to free them. In return, the Totonac king picked twelve hundred of his men to join the Spanish as warriors and porters.[9]

THE ROAD TO MEXICO

The route led upward into the windswept land of the Tlaxcalan. Cortés tried to enlist them, too. The Tlaxcalans, however, chose to test the white men in battle. Badly outnumbered, the Spanish balanced the odds with their superior weapons and tactics. The three weeks of fighting that followed cost both sides dearly. By the time the Spanish had beaten back the final assault, one soldier in six lay dead or wounded. The Tlaxcalans counted their own heavy losses and agreed to join forces with the Spanish.[10]

Cortés received a warm welcome when the column reached Cholula. The Tlaxcalans urged caution, for they knew that the holy city was loyal to Montezuma. A few days later, a friendly local woman warned Malinche that an attack was coming. When Cortés heard the news, he invited many of the city's nobles and warriors to meet with him. Once the plot was confirmed, he ordered his men to attack the unarmed crowd. Hearing the loud musket fire, the Tlaxcalans poured into the city and finished the slaughter.[11]

As the days went by, Cortés and Montezuma traded messages and gifts. At first, the emperor insisted that Cortés was not welcome at Tenochtitlán. After Cholula fell, Montezuma had a change of heart. One theory suggests that he feared Cortés was related to a god named Quetzalcoatl. In Aztec legend, the bearded, light-skinned god was said to have sailed into the eastern sea on a raft of serpents. Before he left, he vowed to return in what the Aztec calendar called a One-Reed year. Cortés had come from the east—and 1519 was a One-Reed year.

A second theory argues that Montezuma planned to spring a trap. Once the Spanish marched the hundred-plus miles to his capital, he could have turned his hordes of warriors loose on them. A third theory suggests that Montezuma hoped the Spanish truly had come to trade. What if he met them and filled their pockets with gold? With their greed satisfied, they might be content to leave.[12]

A stone carving of Quetzalcoatl, the Feathered Serpent. One theory suggests that Montezuma believed Cortés was related to the Aztec god, and because of this, he allowed the Spaniard to enter Tenochtitlán.

CORTÉS ENTERS TENOCHTITLÁN

On November 8, Cortés and his soldiers reached Tenochtitlán. The sight of the Aztec's island capital filled the Spanish with wonder. The great stone city was laced with canals, bridges, and floating gardens. Wide causeways led to an inner zone of temples, palaces, and broad plazas. Home to more than two hundred thousand people, Tenochtitlán was larger than most European cities. In 1519, only Paris and Constantinople, with three hundred thousand people, were larger.[13]

Crowds gathered as Cortés and his men neared the city gates. Carried on a litter by his nobles, Montezuma emerged to meet them. When he stepped down, Cortés advanced to greet him. After an exchange of gifts, the Spaniard stepped forward, as if to embrace his host. Quickly, two Aztec nobles stepped in and pulled the stranger back. Only a select few were allowed to touch the emperor.

Bernardino de Sahagún, a Franciscan missionary, later spoke to the Aztecs who witnessed the meeting. If their reports are true, Montezuma had not yet decided how to handle Cortés. He wanted to be rid of these light-skinned visitors—but first he wanted to learn the secrets of their godlike powers. Also, what if Quetzalcoatl *had* returned? Montezuma seems to have chosen to play it safe.

Cortés Describes the Wonders of Tenochtitlán

Cortés sent several long reports to King Charles. In a letter dated October 30, 1520, he described the marvels of the Aztec capital:

This great city of Tenochtitlán is situated in this salt lake. . . . The city is as large as Seville or Cordova; its [main] streets . . . are very wide and straight. Some of these . . . are half land and half water, and are navigated by canoes. . . . All the streets have openings [spanned by wide, strong wooden bridges]. . . .

This city has . . . one public square twice as large as that of the city of Salamanca. . . . [There] are daily assembled more than sixty-thousand souls, engaged in buying and selling; and where are found . . . articles of food, as well as jewels of gold and silver, lead, brass, copper, tin, precious stones, bones, shells, snails, and feathers. . . .

Among [the city's] temples there is one which . . . [has] room enough for a town of five hundred families. . . . Every chapel . . . is dedicated to a particular idol, to which they pay their devotions. If . . . ill-treated, [the gods] would . . . withhold their gifts, and . . . the people would . . . perish.[14]

In his book, Bernardino de Sahagún described the historic moment:

"Lord, you have reached your destination," Montezuma said as Malinche translated. "You have arrived to take possession of your throne. . . . This is what our kings and those who ruled this your city told us: that you would come to assume your rightful place. . . . Welcome to your kingdom, lords!"

Cortés replied, "Be glad, Montezuma. Fear nothing. We love you greatly. Our heart rejoices. . . . We have reached your house in Tenochtitlán. Hear what we say with an easy mind."

Then, Sahagún writes, ". . . they took one another by the hand, and their followers did likewise."[15]

At first, all seemed well. Montezuma housed his guests in his father's Axayacatl Palace. Aztec nobles took the soldiers on tours of the city's fine palaces, markets, gardens, and zoo. Even so, the Spanish were uneasy. They could scarcely believe the horrors they saw at the temple of Huitzilo-pochtli. Each day, priests honored the god of war by ripping the hearts from helpless victims.

Cortés lectured Montezuma on the need to convert to the Christian faith. As a first step, he asked the emperor to replace the Aztec idols with statues of the saints. Montezuma refused, but he offered Cortés a deal. Leave the idols, he said, and

Cortés kneels before the Aztec Emperor Montezuma upon his reception in Tenochtitlán.

place your Christian statues nearby. Cortés agreed that this was a good first step. While the two men bargained, the Spanish were fortifying the palace and building a chapel. Their labor was rewarded when they broke through a wall and found a room filled with gold and jewels.[16]

As the days slipped past, the Aztecs began to lose patience. Montezuma's refusal to confront Cortés confused his people. Sensing the change, a group of worried Spaniards approached Cortés. "If we want to preserve our lives," they told him, "we must seize Montezuma."[17]

A ROLL OF THE DICE

Cortés soon found an excuse to take this gamble. Word reached him from Veracruz that Aztec warriors had killed some of his soldiers. The next morning, Cortés led a troop of armed soldiers to Montezuma's throne room. Angrily, he blamed the emperor for the deaths. When Montezuma denied the charge, Cortés ordered the emperor to stay with him "as a guest."

Montezuma seemed ready to fly into a rage. He shrank back when a Spanish captain drew his sword. At that point, Cortés stepped forward. Once the killers are punished, he vowed, Montezuma could return to his throne. With that, the emperor meekly allowed the soldiers to lead him back to their quarters.

xaltelolco.

When Cortés spoke with Montezuma, Malinche served as a translator. This drawing shows Cortés seated, with Malinche standing next to him, during a meeting with Montezuma.

Cortés ordered his men to treat his "guest" with respect. Slowly, with his own servants to care for his needs, Montezuma relaxed. After Cortés executed the men accused of the attacks, he told the emperor that he was free to go. To the dismay of his people, Montezuma chose to stay. He may have believed that he actually was obeying the will of the gods.[18]

By now it was April 1520. With Montezuma's blessing, the Spanish helped themselves to a vast store of Aztec gold. They also urged the emperor to embrace the Christian faith, but with very little success. Cortés did talk Montezuma into letting his men remove the great stone idols from the

Montezuma:
The Man and the Ruler

History suggests that Montezuma failed his people, both as a man and as a ruler. How else can one explain the fall of his great empire?

Aztec records tend to disagree. The *Codex Mendoza* says that Montezuma "was by nature wise, . . . skilled in all the arts, civil as well as military." His subjects admired him for "his gravity, demeanor, and power."

Montezuma (his name means "the Angry Lord") came to the throne in 1502. Tall and muscular, he was honored for his feats in battle. The *Codex Mendoza* credits him with more than forty conquests. His victories over Cempoala and the Tlaxcalan came back to haunt him. The two cities joined forces with Cortés in hopes of shaking off Aztec rule.

Did Montezuma believe that Cortés was the god Quetzal-coatl? Perhaps he did, but no one can be certain. Montezuma, like all the Aztecs, did believe that Quetzalcoatl would return to reclaim his throne. All through the early 1500s, a series of ominous signs had bolstered that belief. The signs included a lightning strike on a temple, a fiery comet—and the fact that Cortés arrived in a One-Reed year.

Captive to his own doubts, Montezuma welcomed Cortés into Tenochtitlán. In doing so, he set the stage for the collapse of his kingdom.[19]

During the early 1500s, a series of ominous signs led the Aztecs to believe that Quetzalcoatl was returning to reclaim his throne. One of these signs was a comet flying across the sky. This illustration depicts Montezuma watching the fiery comet pass overhead.

main temple. This act dismayed the Aztec priests. Huitzilopochtli, they said, would surely let the corn wither in the fields. In response, Cortés and his men prayed for rain—and rejoiced when the rains began to fall. Montezuma was not impressed. He told Cortés that the gods were angry—and so were his people. If the Spanish did not leave, he warned, they would all be killed.[20]

While Cortés weighed the threat, couriers arrived from the coast. Their scrolls pictured Spanish ships, nine hundred soldiers, and eighty horses. At first, Cortés welcomed the news. With this new force behind him, he might yet conquer Mexico. His joy faded when he learned that Velázquez had dispatched the expedition. Its task was to complete the conquest and to bring Cortés home in chains.[21]

Chapter 4

"Fortune Always Favors the Bold"

Faced

with the threat of arrest, Cortés had to act. Leaving Pedro de Alvarado and 140 men to protect the palace, he led the rest of his army eastward. Along the way, a horseman met him with a message. In the note, Panfilo de Narváez, the expedition's leader, offered to spare Cortés—if he laid down his arms. In his reply, Cortés coolly warned his rival that it was he who should surrender.[1]

Narváez, the horseman said, had angered his soldiers by not sharing the gifts he received from Montezuma. As a result, the soldiers were ready to listen when Cortés sent Father Olmedo to talk to them. The priest gave the men some Aztec gold as proof that Cortés treated all of his soldiers fairly. Narváez, it turned out, was arrogant as well as selfish. Cortés, he scoffed, would not dare attack his superior force.

Never one to worry about the odds, Cortés did exactly that. After crossing a rain-swollen river, his men stormed the camp in the dead of night. Roused from sleep, the defenders put up only a brief struggle. Narváez might have rallied them, but one of the attackers put him out of action with a pike thrust. When the attack ended, the new-comers gladly switched sides.[2]

Cortés had little time to enjoy his triumph. A message from Tenochtitlán warned him that the Aztecs had broken the truce.

THE DEATH OF MONTEZUMA

After a hurried march, Cortés led a thousand sol-diers, a hundred horsemen, and eight thousand Tlaxcalans into a silent city. Everywhere he looked he saw burned-out buildings and shattered bridges. When Cortés reached the Axayacatl Palace, Alva-rado explained that he had allowed the Aztecs to hold a festival. As the celebration peaked, the sight of so many nobles doing the Serpent Dance alarmed Alvarado. Even though the dancers were unarmed, he ordered an attack. Many nobles died in the massacre that followed—and the city rose up to take revenge.[3]

Cortés saw at once that the danger was real. The Aztecs had cut off all food and water and had closed the public market. He ordered Montezuma, who was still his captive, to reopen the market. The emperor said he could not do so unless he was set free. To buy time, Cortés freed Montezuma's brother, Cuitlahuac. The move backfired. A few days later, the fierce young warrior led a massive attack on the palace.

Diego Velázquez dispatched Panfilo de Narváez and an army to complete the conquest of Mexico and to bring home Cortés in chains. The battle between Cortés and Narváez is shown in this sixteenth-century illustration.

A fold-out from a book published in 1524 shows a map of Tenochtitlán and the Gulf of Mexico (left) that was based on accounts furnished by members of Cortés's expedition. When Cortés returned to Tenochtitlán after defeating Narváez, he found the capital in turmoil.

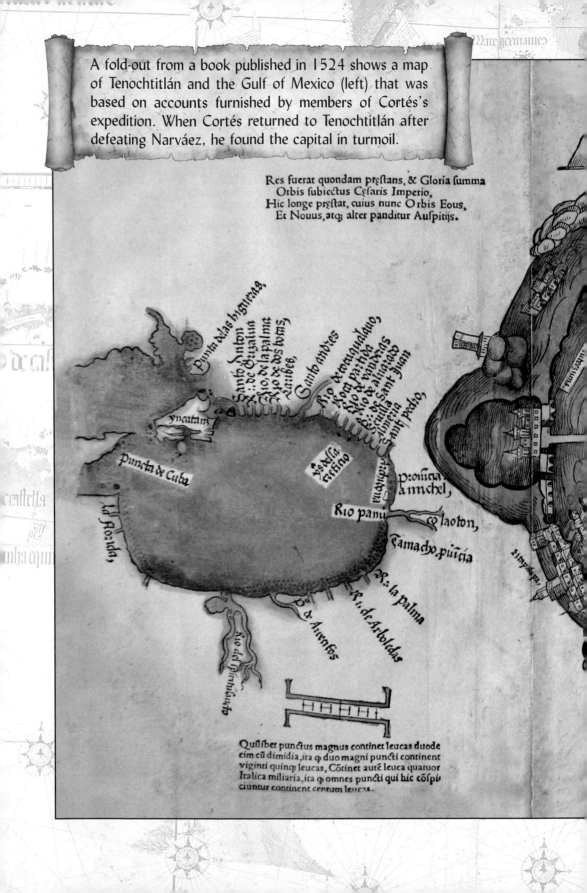

Res fuerat quondam pręstans, & Gloria summa
Orbis subiectus Cęsaris Imperio,
Hic longe pręstat, cuius nunc Orbis Eous,
Et Nouus, atq; alter panditur Auspitijs.

Quilibet punctus magnus continet leucas duode
cim cū dimidia, ita q̃ duo magni puncti continent
viginti quinq; leucas, Cōtinet autē leuca quatuor
Italica miliaria, ita q̃ omnes puncti qui hic cōspi
ciuntur continent centum leucas.

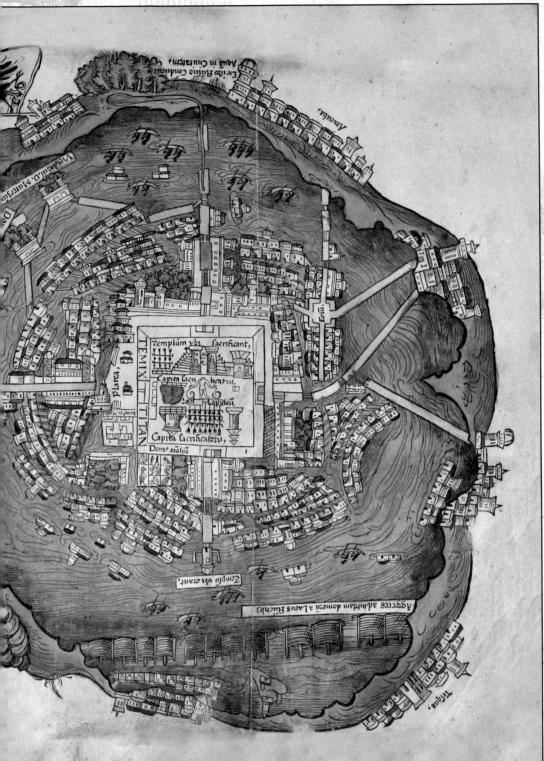

Ex viuo fluuio Conducit
Aqua in Ciuitatem,

Amaxa

Templum vbi sacrificant,

TEMIXTITLAN

Capita sacrificatoru,

ædi F Capitali

PLATEA

Capita sacrificatoru,

Domo aialiu

Templu vbi orant,

Aggeres Adhibitam domos a Lacus Fluctib:

Bernal Díaz later described the ferocity of the fighting: "Neither cannon, muskets nor crossbows were of any avail, nor hand-to-hand combat, nor the slaughter of thirty or forty of them, . . . they still fought on."[4]

As the battle raged, Cortés asked Montezuma to quiet his people. Guarded by his soldiers, the emperor spoke from a wall above the street. He told the restless crowd that the Spanish would leave if they put down their weapons. Enraged, the priests and nobles called the emperor a traitor and hurled stones at him. Montezuma collapsed when one of the stones struck him on the temple. The guards carried the fallen emperor back to his rooms. A doctor did his best to treat the wound. Montezuma, however, ripped off the dressings. Three days later he was dead.[5]

LA NOCHE TRISTE— THE SAD NIGHT

As the siege dragged on, lookouts reported more bad news. The Aztecs, they said, were pulling down the bridges on the best escape route. Men on horseback could leap or swim the gaps in the Tacuba causeway, but not the foot soldiers. Cortés quickly put his men to work building a portable bridge.

On June 30, 1520, the captain-general called his men to a meeting. The soldiers' eyes lit up when they saw Montezuma's treasure piled beside him. After setting aside the king's fifth and his own share, he told the men to divide the rest. His veterans took mostly lightweight gems and jade. When their turn came, Narváez's men grabbed all the gold they could carry.[6]

That night, cloaked by a light rain, Cortés led his men onto the causeway. When they reached the first gap, the Tlaxcalan porters dropped the wooden bridge into place. An Aztec woman saw them and her screams awoke the city. After the column tramped across the bridge, the porters tried to pick it up again. It was stuck fast. Dodging

Cortés and his soldiers tried to flee Tenochtitlán after Montezuma's death. The bloody battle that ensued came to be known as *La Noche Triste*.

a hail of Aztec arrows, the men raced on to the next gap. Cortés and his horsemen scrambled across easily enough. The first wave of foot soldiers stopped at the edge to look for a way to cross. The delay was fatal. The crowd surging from behind pushed many of the men into the water. Weighed down by gold, scores of Narváez's soldiers drowned. As López de Gómara later wrote: "Those who died, died rich, and their God killed them."[7]

The Aztecs attacked on foot and in canoes. When they took prisoners, they dragged their captives off to be sacrificed. Alvarado saved himself by using his spear to vault across one of the gaps. At last, the causeway behind them, the survivors stumbled on toward Tacuba. Some eight hundred Spaniards and four thousand Tlaxcalans died that night. Most of Montezuma's treasure vanished into the lake.

When he reached Tacuba, Cortés sat under a tree and wept. Malinche attempted to comfort him by tending his wounds. It was, indeed, *La Noche Triste*.[8]

THE TURNAROUND

Certain of victory, the Aztecs pulled back to give thanks to their gods. The delay gave Cortés time to press on toward Tlaxcala. Wounded men who could not keep up were left behind to die. By the sixth day, the survivors were more hopeful. Then, as they headed down into the Valley of Otumba, their spirits sagged. Waiting below was a vast army of Aztecs and their Otomí allies. Retreat was not an option.

Cortés led his soldiers into the valley and prepared for battle. When the fighting began, Spanish gunners and swordsmen beat back wave after wave of attackers. Many hours passed, and still the battle raged. Late in the day, a weary Cortés spotted the plumed headdress of the Aztec leader. Followed by five horsemen, he spurred his way through the milling warriors. When he reached the cacique, Cortés knocked the man down. One of his captains finished the job with a lance thrust. Leaderless now, the Indians broke and ran.[9]

Cortés received a warm welcome when his ragged column reached Tlaxcala. Even so, a lesser man might have called off the struggle. Two of Cortés's fingers had been crushed and his head was bleeding badly from a deep gash. His battered army was short of gunpowder, cannon, and crossbows. Some of the men begged him to return to Cuba. Cortés won them back by appealing to their pride: "Do you want it said that 'Cortés and his men retreated when they were safe, well fed, and in no danger?' God forbid!"[10]

In the weeks that followed, Cortés rebuilt his army. Morale improved when fresh soldiers, guns, and horses arrived from Vera Cruz. The Indians from the nearby cities were flocking to Cortés's banner, too. These warriors had little love for the Spanish, but they hated the Aztecs even more. To train his recruits, Cortés mounted raids against cities allied with the Aztecs.

Back at Tlaxcala, carpenters were shaping hulls and masts for thirteen brigantines. Once launched, the swift little boats would allow Cortés to attack Tenochtitlán by land and by water. "Fortune," he assured his men, "always favors the bold."[11]

THE SIEGE OF TENOCHTITLÁN

On December 28, 1520, Cortés led 40 horsemen, 550 foot soldiers, and 20,000 Tlaxcalans toward Tenochtitlán.[12] He now had a new and deadly ally,

AN EPIDEMIC SWEEPS MEXICO

One of Panfilo de Narváez's sailors carried the smallpox virus to Mexico. Smallpox had ravaged Europe for centuries, and the Spanish had developed some resistance to the disease. The Indians had little or no immunity. Once stricken, many tried to ease the pain by going to one of their public baths. The pools quickly passed on the virus to other bathers.[13]

The Aztecs described the sickness as covering their bodies "with agonizing sores." The sick "could only lie on their beds like corpses. . . . If they did move their bodies, they screamed with pain." The few who did survive did not escape unmarked. Wherever a sore broke through the skin, "it gouged an ugly pockmark."[14]

In this Aztec drawing from 1521, Cortés and a Tlaxcalan chief supervise the construction of brigantines used during the siege of Tenochtitlán. Once the brigantines were launched, Cortés could attack the city by land and water.

for smallpox ravaged the city. One of the disease's first victims was Cuitlahuac, the new emperor. His nephew, Cuauhtémoc, took his place.[15]

Cortés and his army first targeted a city on Lake Texcoco's eastern shore. Instead of fighting, the people of Texcoco opened their gates to him. When Cuauhtémoc ignored his offer to make peace, Cortés burned several nearby cities. Late in April 1521, work crews launched the two-masted brigantines they had carried piece by piece from Tlaxcala.

Once his men had learned to handle their new ships, Cortés struck. On May 26, 1521, a raiding party wrecked the aqueduct that supplied the capital city's drinking water. Two other battle groups sealed off the remaining escape routes. On June 1, the crews boarded the brigantines and set sail. Warned by lookouts, a fleet of Aztec war canoes moved out to meet them.

As wind gusts filled their sails, the sturdy brigantines rammed the oncoming fleet. Dozens of canoes splintered and sank. The Aztecs were far from beaten, but Cortés had gained control of the causeways. The defenders were forced to depend on canoes to ferry in food and water. To combat

A FAILURE OF TECHNOLOGY

Without guns, swords, and armor, the Spanish might well have lost the battle for Tenochtitlán. Even so, as the siege dragged on, Cortés's worries mounted. His Indian allies were deserting, and his stock of gunpowder was running low.

At that point, one of his men offered to build a giant catapult. Once the machine was constructed, he said, it would crush the defenders under a barrage of large, heavy stones. Cortés supplied the amateur engineer with timbers, ropes, wheels, and workmen. Before long, the great catapult was ready. Soldiers wrestled a large stone into place and prepared to fire. From the nearby buildings, Aztec warriors watched in silent awe.

Cortés gave the command. The firing arm snapped forward and hurled the stone into the sky. Instead of arcing toward its target, the missile seemed to pause at the top of its flight. Then it plunged straight down. As the soldiers scattered, the stone smashed the catapult to bits. Cheered by the debacle, the Aztec defenders shouted insults at their downcast foes.[16]

the brigantines, they drove sharp stakes into the lake bed. Spanish gunners fought back by raking the causeways with cannon fire.[17]

The seesaw battle raged for weeks. Each time the Spanish broke through to the heart of the city, Aztec warriors drove them back. The Aztecs took prisoners whenever they could. Later, the priests sacrificed the luckless captives on bloodstained altars.[18] As Tenochtitlán burned and the fighting dragged on, casualties mounted. Spanish soldiers complained that they could not move "without treading on the bodies . . . of dead Indians."[19]

On the night of August 11, a great fireball blazed across the sky. The Aztecs, worn down by sickness and hunger, lost heart. In their eycs, the meteor signaled their god's displeasure. Two days later, Cuauhtémoc surrendered. The Spanish relished their triumph, but where was Montezuma's gold? After a careful search failed to find the treasure, Cortés allowed his men to hold Cuauhtémoc's feet to the fire. To their dismay, the emperor would not—or could not—answer their questions. The lost riches were never found.[20]

🌐 BUILDING NEW SPAIN

Cortés wrote a long letter to King Charles I to report his great triumph. In a typical passage, he described one of his strategies:

When the time came I gave orders for my men to retreat in good order and for the horsemen to begin a charge . . . but to pretend to be afraid and stop short. . . . The enemy pursued [the retreating soldiers] with such wild cries that one might have thought they had conquered the world. The . . . horsemen made as if to attack . . . and then withdrew suddenly. . . . When we saw the Spaniards pass in front of us, . . . we knew it was time to emerge; and so . . . we charged up the square, spearing them, cutting them down and overtaking many of them, who were then slain by our [Indian] allies. . . . That night our allies dined sumptuously, for all those they had killed were sliced up and eaten.[21]

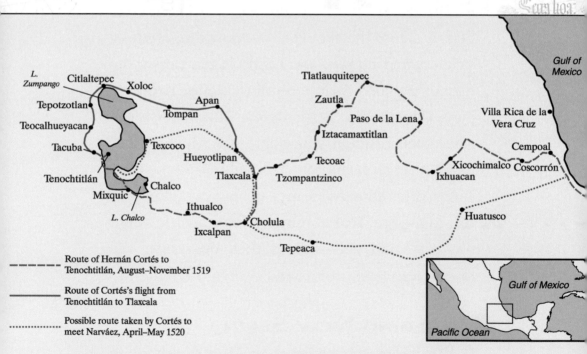

The road to conquest took Cortés to many places in Mexico. This map shows some of the routes he took and the cities he visited.

After he read the report, Cortés believed, the king would grant him a title and the post of governor. While he waited for a reply, he put his men to work rebuilding the capital and searching for gold. Keeping his soldiers busy, Cortés hoped, would calm their anger over the division of the spoils. After he took out the king's fifth and his own share, the average soldier received only fifty to sixty pesos. The meager payout was barely enough to buy a new sword.[22]

King Charles I confirmed Cortés as captain-general of New Spain in 1522. Later, he tacked on the title of marqués of the Oaxaca Valley. Elated by his new title, Cortés switched easily from the role of warrior to that of builder. Tenochtitlán, splendidly rebuilt and renamed Mexico City, became Spain's New World capital. Miners opened rich silver mines and settlers arrived to start farms and ranches. Cortés introduced new crops (sugarcane and wheat) and livestock (cattle and sheep). By 1528, New Spain ranked as the crown's richest colony.

As the colony grew, priests labored to convert the Indians to Christianity. The turning point came in 1531. That was when the newly baptized Juan Diego reported that a dark-skinned Virgin Mary had appeared to him on Tepeyac Hill. When his bishop asked for proof, Diego returned three days later. Even though it was December, his cloak was filled with roses—and bore a portrait of Mary. As news of the "miracle of the Virgin of Guadalupe" spread, more and more Indians embraced the Catholic faith.[23]

YEARS OF GLORY, YEARS OF ANGUISH

Hernán Cortés died long ago, but he is still the subject of bitter debate. Even in his lifetime, he was both loved and hated. Some called him a heartless butcher. Compared to Francisco Pizarro's savage treatment of the Incas, however, Cortés was an "angel of mercy." When he returned in 1530 from a visit to Spain, Spaniards and Indians alike gave him a hero's welcome.[24]

Building New Spain was one of the captain-general's tasks. Cortés also set out to map his new domain. On one voyage, he discovered Baja California and gave his name to the Sea of Cortés. His captains led expeditions that reached as far south as Honduras and Guatemala.

Cortés's troubles grew along with his fame. His wife, Catalina, joined him at about the same time Malinche gave birth to his son, Martín. Three months later, Cortés and Catalina had an argument at a banquet—and she died that same night. His enemies charged him with murder, but he was never brought to trial. In 1528, after two more suspicious deaths, King Charles called Cortés back to Spain. But before he sailed, Cortés filled his ship with New World treasures and exotic animals. The gifts he brought back pleased the king, who confirmed the captain-general's lands and titles.

Even though Cortés received a warm welcome upon his return to Spain, his power was slipping. He was forced to spend a lot of his time defending himself. In 1540, he sailed back to Spain to argue his case before the court. This time, King Charles ignored him. Cortés hung on, hoping to return to favor, but to no avail. Ill and depressed, he died on December 2, 1547, and was laid to rest in a family plot. Several years later, his body was shipped to Mexico for burial, as he had requested.[25]

In modern times, writers have both praised and criticized Hernán Cortés. Historian Lesley Byrd Simpson was an admirer. "The Kingdom of New Spain," Simpson wrote, "was his vision and very largely his accomplishment."[26]

Chapter 5
The Legacy of Conquest

The Spanish who conquered Mexico saw little reason to respect their vanquished foes. As passions cooled, a few priests and scholars did begin to study the fallen cultures. Only an advanced culture, they realized, could have built the land's great cities.

Historians date the birth of Mexico's high cultures at around A.D. 300. That was when the Maya built their magnificent stone cities in Yucatán. In the central highlands, the Olmec, the Toltec, and the Aztec rose to power one after another. The three cultures worshipped gods of the sun, moon, rain, and many other natural elements. They also developed written languages and calendars. Skilled craftsmen built cities that rivaled Europe's finest. As proof, the massive Pyramid of the Sun still towers above the ancient religious center of Teotihuacán.[1]

The Toltec displaced the ruling Olmec in the ninth century. The newcomers built an empire whose crown jewel was the city of Tula. Grander than Teotihuacán, Tula's palaces were adorned with gold, jewels, and seashells. As the years passed, one

The Pyramid of the Sun in Teotihuacán. Many people still visit this ancient religious center today.

group of Toltecs embraced a fierce war god called Tezcatlipoca. To win the god's favor, these followers embraced the practice of human sacrifice. A second group worshipped the plumed serpent, Quetzalcoatl. To please this gentle god, the priests sacrificed butterflies and snakes. At last, weakened by division and famine, the Toltecs fell victim to a new wave of invaders.[2]

THE AZTECS ENTER THE VALLEY OF MEXICO

The northern tribes that scattered the Toltec were known as the Chichimec. As time passed, these nomads set up their own city-states. Some of the cities became allies. Others, hungry for land and power, warred on their neighbors. In the 1100s, the most ruthless Chichimec of all arrived. They called themselves the Mexica, but history knows them as the Aztecs.

Aztec warriors often hired out to fight for the older, richer city-states. When not at war, they hunted and fished. Over time, they also learned how to farm. In the early 1300s, their search for a home led them to Lake Texcoco. It was there, legend says, that a priest saw an eagle with a snake in its beak perched on a cactus. This was a sign, the priest said, that the Aztecs were finally home at last.[3] Mexico later adopted that image as its national coat of arms. The eagle also is featured on the nation's flag.

During the next thirty years, the Aztecs built their splendid island city. When it was finished, Tenochtitlán was home to stone temples, palaces, markets, and causeways. To feed the bustling city, farmers built floating gardens called *chinampas*. Thanks to the moist, rich soil, the gardens yielded three crops of maize (corn) a year. Happy and secure in their new home, the Aztecs then began

building an empire. By the 1500s, their domain stretched from the Gulf coast to the Pacific.[4]

A CULTURE BUILT ON HUMAN SACRIFICE

The Aztecs lived under strict religious and social codes. Drawing on the Toltec beliefs, their priests nourished the gods with human hearts. That practice climaxed at the end of each fifty-two year cycle. The New Fire Ceremony began with the sacrifice of captive warriors. Then the priests carried the freshly kindled fire to Huitzilopochtli's temple in Tenochtitlán. When the people saw the fire, they "all were quieted in their hearts."[5]

Each Aztec knew his or her place in society. The upper classes, known as the *pipiltin,* traced their ancestry to an early Toltec ruler. Schooled as priests, war leaders, and high officials, these nobles ruled the empire. Montezuma, like the emperors before him, was chosen from the ranks of the *pipiltin*. The Aztec middle class—the *macehualtin*—toiled as farmers, soldiers, merchants, and craftsmen. The hardest labor was assigned to the working class, the *mayeques*. Talented *mayeques* sometimes rose to join the middle class. Prisoners of war who were not sacrificed on the altars were kept as slaves.[6]

The Aztec way of life collapsed when Tenochtitlán fell. The people lived on, but they were now

THE AZTECS FIGHT A "FLOWERY WAR"

In 1424, a newly crowned Aztec ruler, Itzcóatl, had to make a tough choice. Threatened by the city-state of Azcapotzalco, Itzcóatl would have to fight or yield. At first, Itzcóatl and his nobles leaned toward surrender. Then young Tlacaélel stepped forward. "Sire, what is this?" he challenged. "Let some means be sought for our defense and our honor."

Heartened by his words, the Aztecs fought hard—and won. Tlacaélel then worked with Itzcóatl to rewrite their people's history. The new version invented a close bond with the fallen Toltec culture and its religion. Most notably, Tlacaélel raised Huitzilopochtli to a lofty rank. To please the war god, he taught, the Aztecs must quench his thirst for human blood. If they did so, they could be sure that the sun would rise each day.

The Aztecs built a great temple to Huitzilopochtli in Tenochtitlán. To keep the altars supplied with hearts and blood, Tlacaélel devised the "flowery war." These wars were fought for the sole purpose of taking prisoners. "Our god will feed himself with [the captives]," Tlacaélel said. It will be "as though he were eating warm tortillas . . . straight out of the oven."

"Flowery wars" kept the sacrificial altars busy. The wars also aroused deep hatreds in the cities that came under attack. A century later, the Aztecs paid a heavy price for using the tactic. The support Cortés received from the Tlaxcalan and other Aztec-hating cities was crucial to the conquest.[7]

captive to the will of the Spanish *conquistadores*. A lament, written around 1523, gives voice to their grief:

> Weep, my people:
> know that with these disasters
> we have lost the Mexican nation.
> The water has turned bitter,
> our food is bitter!
> These are the acts of the Giver of Life.[8]

SPAIN REBUILDS MEXICO IN ITS OWN IMAGE

The 1500s were heady times for the people of Spain. Conquistadores added great chunks of the New World to their empire. To rule the vast region, the Spaniards set up two viceroyalties. The viceroy of New Spain governed Mexico, most of Central America, and the islands of the Caribbean. From Panama south to Patagonia, the viceroy of Peru governed the South American colonies.[9]

Spaniards by the thousands set sail for Mexico during the 1500s. As they had in Cuba, crown officials welcomed them with land grants. In return for the use of Indian labor, the *encomenderos* (landowners) agreed to protect and Christianize their workers. The system led to so many abuses that Spain replaced it with the *repartimiento* in the 1550s. The new plan cut the Indian workers' labor "debt" to forty-five days a year. That should have freed the Indians to grow their own crops on the

MEXICO.

MEXICO REGIA
ET CELEBRIS
HISPANIÆ NO-
VAE CIVITAS.

Cum Priuilegio

This drawing of Mexico City in the sixteenth century was probably based on sketches from Cortés's expedition. Built on the ruins of Tenochtitlán, Mexico City became the capital of the colony of New Spain.

ejidos (communal farms) set aside for them. Many landowners, however, still treated their workers like slaves. Wracked by disease, hunger, and over-work, the native population fell sharply.[10]

Mexican society split into rigid social classes. The *gachupines* (whites born in Spain) topped the social pyramid. Close behind came the *criollos* (whites born in New Spain to Spanish parents). These two groups controlled the lion's share of Mexico's land, wealth, and power. Next came the *mestizos* (people born to Spanish and Indian par-ents). The Indians, plus slaves shipped in from Africa, toiled at the bottom of the pyramid. The unifying force of the Catholic Church helped keep the social order intact.[11]

MEXICO WINS ITS INDEPENDENCE

As the decades passed, Spain's power dwindled. Wars with England and France stripped away many of its colonies. In Mexico, ties to a distant mother country began to weaken. Criollos and mestizos alike were denied high government jobs. Inspired by the American and French revolutions, many Mexicans began to dream of freedom and self-rule.[12]

Independence did not come easily in Mexico. Government officials loyal to Spain used the army to maintain control. Mexico remained peaceful

Father Miguel Hidalgo y Costilla issued his "Grito de Dolores," or his call to rebel, on September 16, 1810. Father Hidalgo stands at the center of this mural urging his fellow Indians and mestizos to fight for Mexican independence.

until September 16, 1810, when Father Miguel Hidalgo y Costilla issued his "Grito de Dolores." Indians and mestizos answered his call to fight for independence. Led by Hidalgo and Ignacio de Allende, the rebels marched on the silver mining city of Guanajuato. The bloody civil war that followed dragged on for a number of years.[13]

Mexico declared its independence in 1824, but freedom did not solve all the nation's problems. During the next fifty years, the presidency changed hands seventy-five times. War with the United States from 1846 to 1848 cost Mexico its claim to lands in the American Southwest. In 1864, the French invaded Mexico and installed the Archduke Maximilian of Austria as the new emperor. Three years later, Benito Juárez led a violent revolt that ended with the death of the ill-fated Austrian. In 1876, Porfirio Díaz won the presidency—and held the post until 1911.

A More Democratic Nation

The gulf between the classes grew wider during the Díaz years. Rich criollos sipped fine wines and sent their children to private schools. The Indians and mestizos who toiled in the fields and factories could only dream of such luxuries. Families survived on meager rations of corn, beans, and rice. Meat was a luxury few could afford, as were schools for the children. When the call came to fight for a better life, the poor felt they had little to lose.

In 1910, Francisco Madero challenged the Díaz dictatorship. His platform called for free elections and a one-term limit for the presidency. Díaz responded by arresting Madero. Released after Díaz won reelection, Madero called on the people to revolt. Lured by dreams of a better life, the countryside took up arms. Emiliano Zapata, a mestizo peasant farmer turned rebel, emerged as

Father Hidalgo and El Grito de Dolores

Mexico observes its Independence Day each September 16. In the capital, Mexico City, the president kicks off the observance by repeating the Grito de Dolores. The waiting crowd responds to his call with rousing shouts of "Viva Mexico!"

El Grito was first given voice in 1810 by Father Miguel Hidalgo y Costilla. Alarmed by the priest's freethinking ways, the church moved him to Dolores, a small parish in central Mexico. Hidalgo, a criollo, was angered by the demotion. Church leaders, he charged, favored priests born in Spain.

While serving in Dolores, Hidalgo joined a debate group. Inspired by the French Revolution, the members talked freely of starting a rebellion. When word of the plan leaked out, the police arrested some of the plotters.

Hidalgo acted quickly when he heard the news. On September 16, 1810, speaking from his pulpit, he raised the Grito. "Long live Our Lady of Guadalupe! Long live Independence!" Hidalgo thundered. His Indian followers added their own battle cry: "Death to the *gachupines!*"

Led by Hidalgo, an army of angry Indians overran the city of Guanajuato. As news of the revolt spread, frightened criollos and gachupines joined forces. Army troops moved in and fought Hidalgo's ragtag troops to a standstill. In February 1811, they arrested the priest and tried him for treason. He was shot on July 31, 1811.

New leaders quickly stepped forward to lead the rebel armies. The fighting dragged on until 1824, when a free Mexico declared itself a republic.[14]

a key leader. His cry of "Tierra y libertad!" ("Land and liberty!") drew thousands of recruits.[15]

The next ten years were marked by widespread chaos. After the revolution drove Díaz from power, a series of power-hungry presidents took his place. A measure of calm returned in 1917 when a congress approved a new constitution. The document offered the people of Mexico some long-sought rights:

- Civil rights for all Mexicans
- Free and fair elections, with presidents held to one six-year term
- A free public education
- Indians empowered to demand the return of *ejido* lands taken from them
- Mining rights reserved to the state
- Workers allowed to join unions and to go on strike[16]

Ninety years later, many of those pledges have been fulfilled. Many Indian farmers, however, are still waiting to reclaim their ancestral lands.

RISE OF THE EZLN

The need for land reform is most acute in the poor southern state of Chiapas. Ever since the 1500s, wealthy ranchers have held much of the state's richest farmland. When the Indians filed claims, the ranchers often bribed officials to ignore them.

THE ZAPATISTAS CAMPAIGN FOR INDIAN RIGHTS

The Zapatista Army of National Liberation (EZLN) chose its name carefully. Mexicans revere their rebel heroes, and Emiliano Zapata ranks high on that list. Calling themselves Zapatistas marks the members as fighters for social justice.

The Zapatistas won the hearts of Indians and mestizos alike with the slogan, "Everything for everyone, and nothing for ourselves." When they take over a village, the Zapatistas set up self-governing *juntas* (councils). A *junta* member holds office for only a few weeks before stepping aside. In this way, everyone has an equal chance to serve. The system also keeps officials from becoming addicted to power.

A sign posted near a highway in Chiapas sums up the EZLN's views. The top half of the sign reads:

> YOU ARE IN ZAPATISTA REBEL TERRITORY. HERE THE PEOPLE GIVE THE ORDERS AND THE GOVERNMENT OBEYS.

The bottom half of the sign lists some of the local rules:

> TRAFFICKING IN WEAPONS, PLANTING OF DRUGS, DRUG USE, ALCOHOLIC BEVERAGES, AND ILLEGAL SALES OF WOOD ARE STRICTLY PROHIBITED. NO TO THE DESTRUCTION OF NATURE!

If Emiliano Zapata were alive today, he would likely join the EZLN. Like their namesake, the Zapatistas march to the battle cry of "Tierra y Libertad!"[17]

A masked Zapatista rebel shouts slogans during a march through San Cristobal de las Casas, Mexico, on September 8, 1997. The Zapatistas were marching to Mexico City to demand support for Indian rights.

The land that was transferred to the *ejidos* often proved to be of little value.

The long-running conflict took center stage on January 1, 1994. That was the day that Mexico joined the United States and Canada in the North American Free Trade Agreement (NAFTA). Under the treaty, trade goods move freely from country to country. City dwellers argued that the treaty would aid Mexico's sluggish economy. Peasant leaders did not agree. Mexico's small farms, they charged, could not compete with American farm exports.

The protests were led by insurgents known as the Zapatista Army of National Liberation (EZLN). When the army moved in with its heavy guns, the EZLN leaders changed tactics. Laying down their guns, they spoke out in the media and on the Internet. "Join us," they cried, "in a peaceful fight for social justice."[18]

One of the EZLN's best-known leaders calls himself Subcomandante Marcos. In public, Marcos wears a black ski mask and a bandolier of red shotgun shells. "El Sub," says the EZLN seeks, "the basic rights of the human: education, housing, health, food, land, good pay, . . . democracy." Those main goals strike sparks with the Mexican people—and in the wider world that once was the Spanish Empire.[19]

Chapter 6

A Dark and Tangled History

From Mexico to Tierra del Fuego, the countries of Latin America often make news. Some of the reports point to hopeful signs of progress. Others paint a bleak picture of social, economic, and political ills. The best reporters dig out stories that help their readers make sense of tangled events.

In 1992, Mexico was marking the anniversary of Columbus's epic voyage. While walking through the town of San Miguel de Allende, writer Tony Cohan passed a stone statue of Columbus. The explorer's head, he was shocked to see, was lying at the base of the statue. During the night, some local mestizos had broken it off. The vandalism, he learned, was meant to protest Mexico's long abuse of its Indians. As the news spread, San Miguel's criollos tried to even the score by laying a wreath at the base of the statue. In their eyes, Mexico's Spanish heritage was a matter of pride, not of shame.[1]

Clearly, Spain's colonial legacy still troubles Latin America.

⬤ "Glory, Gold, and God"

In the 1500s, Hernán Cortés's defeat of the Aztecs set the stage for a wave of Spanish conquests. In Peru, Francisco Pizarro used similar tactics to conquer the Inca Empire. Pizarro began his campaign in 1532 by boldly taking the emperor Atahualpa captive. As ransom, Atahualpa offered the Spanish a room filled with gold and two filled with silver. Pizarro agreed. But when the treasure arrived, he seized it—and then executed the emperor. Leaderless without Atahualpa, the empire collapsed.[2]

A number of similar dramas played out in the years that followed. In South America, conquistadores added the present-day countries of Ecuador, Colombia, and Chile to Spain's empire. In Central America, Spanish troops carved out a long chain of settlements. In time, those colonies became the modern nations of Guatemala, Honduras, Costa Rica, Nicaragua, and Panama. In Brazil, precious metals and Indian workers were in short supply. The early Portuguese settlers took heart when Europe's growing taste for sugar opened a new market. To work the new cane fields, Portugal shipped in boatloads of African slaves.

Once planted, the Spanish empire's colonies grew with amazing speed. Most of the newcomers had little interest in the native peoples, other than to exploit them. They grabbed the best lands and worked them with Indian labor. True to the times of the conquistadores, these gachupines lived for "glory, gold, and God."[3]

A GROWING DISCONTENT

The first English colonists landed at Jamestown in 1607. By that time, 250,000 Spanish and Portuguese settlers were living in the New World.[4] Along with gold, silver, copper, and other metals, the land produced a bounty of new crops. Corn, potatoes, and tomatoes found their way into the diets of the rich and poor. Europeans also prized the dried leaves of the tobacco plant. Smoking or chewing the leaves, they believed, would cure most ills. A drink known as cocoa, brewed from cacao beans, was nearly as popular. Roasted and laced with sugar, the beans also flavored a new sweet called chocolate.

By the 1800s, Latin America was also harvesting bumper crops of discontent. Europe's rulers cruelly exploited the colonies. Merchant captains kept a tight hold on rich trade routes. The Church, focused on saving souls, did very little to promote social justice. When native peoples fought back, Spanish troops rushed in with muskets blazing. Thanks to their weaponry (and aided by diseases such as smallpox), the settlers won most of these battles.

Europe ruled its colonies with an iron hand. For three hundred years, Latin America chafed under rules that forbid the building of factories. The colonists had no choice but to sell their silver, cotton, tobacco, and sugar to the Spaniards. A farmer who needed a new rifle or a better plow was forced to import it. From wealthy criollos to landless mestizos, colonists dreamed of taking control of their futures.[5]

THE INDEPENDENCE MOVEMENT

Latin America's wealthy criollos were the first to strike back. Discontent flamed into open revolt as news of the American Revolution spread south. In Peru, Colombia, and Ecuador, colonists took up arms in the late 1700s. The rebels fought bravely, but Spanish troops crushed the uprisings. The first successful revolt took place on the island of Hispaniola. There, in 1794, Toussaint L'Ouverture and his fellow blacks rebelled against their French masters. After Toussaint died in prison, Jean Jacques Dessalines took charge and finished the job. Haiti declared its independence in 1804.[6]

To many Latin Americans, the message seemed clear. If ill-trained black slaves could defeat a French army, surely their own militias could defeat Spain's troops. The mother country, they knew, had been weakened by wars in Europe. In the end, it was a British attempt to seize Argentina that sparked the wars for independence.

After local criollos helped defeat the British, the colonists launched their own revolts. Paraguay won its freedom in 1811 and Uruguay followed in 1815. Elsewhere, two great generals took command of the colonial armies. José de San Martín freed Argentina in 1816, Chile in 1818, and Peru in 1821. By 1825, under the leadership of Simón Bolívar, Venezuela, Colombia, Ecuador, and Bolivia had thrown off the Spanish yoke. Farther north, the peoples of Mexico and Central America fought and won their own rebellions. By 1821, most of Latin America had embarked on a perilous new journey.[7]

The newly-freed states were poorly prepared for self-rule. Using the United States as a model, many tried to set up democratic systems. All too often, the new governments soon collapsed. In some countries, *caudillos* (dictators) stepped in and took charge. In others, small groups of wealthy criollos and mestizos controlled the levers of power.[8] The former colonies also quarreled with their neighbors. As early as 1825, Argentina and Brazil went to war over land that each claimed as its own. In 1879, Chile won a nitrate-rich strip along the Pacific coast in a war with Bolivia.

Throughout Latin America, the lower classes— needy mestizos, Indians, and blacks—sank deeper into poverty.

Simón Bolívar helped many Latin American countries gain their independence from Spain.

Mexico's Charismatic Caudillo

Independence put Europe's former colonies on the road to self-rule. The United States set a high standard by choosing a strong democratic system. The new Latin American nations, however, sometimes stumbled. Frequently, power-hungry caudillos seized power.

One of the most colorful caudillos was Mexico's Antonio López de Santa Anna. Born into a criollo family in 1794, the young Santa Anna trained as a soldier. He won praise for his courage while fighting for Spain during Mexico's 1810 war for independence. In 1821, Santa Anna switched sides. He became a hero when he crushed a Spanish invasion at Tampico.

In those chaotic years, Santa Anna served as president on at least ten occasions. His longest term lasted just over a year, from 1841 to 1842. One brief stay ended after just ten days. When Texans declared their independence in 1836, Santa Anna led the campaign to put down the rebellion. He won the bloody battle at the Alamo, but was captured at San Jacinto two months later. To free himself, he granted Texas its freedom.

Santa Anna soon bounced back despite the defeat. After losing his leg in a battle with the French at Veracruz, he buried the leg with full military honors. Once again a hero, he was recalled to the presidency. But Santa Anna raised taxes and stuffed his pockets with gold. Forced out of office yet again, he continued to rise and fall in favor. At last, penniless and nearly blind, the "Napoleon of the West" died in 1876.[9]

⬤ A Long, Uphill Road

Writer Alphonse Karr says that "the more things change, the more they stay the same." Life in today's Latin America testifies to the truth of his statement. Three Indian *campesinos*, or peasant farmers, responded to a writer's questions in 1994. The year, however, could well have been 1794 or 1894. Like the Aztecs, these men work their fields with pointed sticks.

"If you could have anything you wished for, what would it be?" Alma Guillermoprieto asked.

"Some good farm equipment," one campesino answered.

"A dignified life with a little rest," the second man added.

"And a school, so the children can be whatever they like when they grow up," the third man said.[10]

Those melancholy wishes underscore the grim heritage that Spain left to its New World colonies. To measure that bequest, economists add up all the goods and services produced by a country (the Gross National Product, or GNP). Latin America's lagging GNP helps explain the plight of the three campesinos:

- In terms of population and land area, Latin America is roughly twice the size of the United States.

- The U.S. GNP, however, is six times larger than the combined GNPs of all its Latin American neighbors.[11]

Clearly, long years of Spanish misrule left a lasting imprint. Latin America's history of social and economic injustice plays out daily in cities, towns, and villages. Democracy and free markets are taking root, but the road ahead is rocky. All too often, dictatorships have run roughshod over the people's democratic hopes.

Is there any hope? In the 1920s, José Vasconcelos helped Mexico fix some of its problems. As minister of education, Vasconcelos built schools and trained teachers. Almost at once, the illiteracy rate began to go down. To further his crusade, Vasconcelos encouraged artists, musicians, and writers to celebrate their cultural heritage. Latin Americans, he said, must "cease being [Europe's] spiritual colonies." In our art, music, dance, and books, Vasconcelos told his people, we can see "the birth of the Latin American soul."[12]

OLD HATREDS DIE HARD

Inspired by leaders such as Vasconcelos, Latin Americans take pride in their heroes. Mexico, for example, honors Cuauhtémoc, Father Hidalgo, Zapata, and a long list of other notables. One well-known name, however, is missing from that list. Even today, centuries after the fall of Tenochtitlán,

A view of downtown Mexico City. Cortés's body lies in a crypt in one of the city's churches, but few people visit it.

most Mexicans view Hernán Cortés as a cruel oppressor. Artists, if they depict Cortés at all, tend to paint him as a deformed, evil man.

This loathing shows few signs of easing. No monument marks the beach near Veracruz where Cortés landed in 1519. The conquistador's body lies in a crypt in the Templo de Jesús in Mexico City—but few Mexicans know it is there. In 1823, during the war for independence, rebels plotted to destroy his remains. The Cortés family foiled the plan by hiding the coffin. Today, fearful that some-one will blow up the crypt, the police restrict access to the site. During the 1990s, the city of Coyoacan installed a public fountain that honored Cortés, Malinche, and their son, Martín. Instead of building civic pride, the project touched off violent protests. Rather than risk a riot, the city removed the fountain.[13]

Despite this history of neglect, Cortés is not entirely ignored. His crypt is marked by a bust carved by sculptor Manuel Tolsá. A second site, in the mountains above Mexico City, is known as Paso de Cortés (Cortés Pass). A brass plaque at the summit marks the route the Spanish took on their march to Tenochtitlán.[14]

As the dearth of honors suggests, the average Mexican has no love for either Cortés or Malinche. Peter Rashkin once told a Mexican friend that he rather admired the conquistador. His friend was not amused. "So," she snapped, "you admire a thief and a torturer?"[15]

Asked about Malinche, painter Rina Lazo was just as curt. "For Mexico to create a monument to La Malinche," she said, "would be like giving an award to the [pilot] who dropped the atomic bomb on Hiroshima."[16]

These harsh judgments may soften someday . . . but history will always view Cortés as a highly controversial figure.

Chapter Notes

Chapter 1. A Conquistador Comes of Age

1. William Weber Johnson, *Cortés* (Boston: Little, Brown & Co., 1975), p. 14.

2. Hugh Thomas, *Conquest: Montezuma, Cortés, and the Fall of Old Mexico* (New York: Simon & Schuster, 1993), p. 132.

3. Jon Manchip White, *Cortés and the Downfall of the Aztec Empire* (New York: St. Martin's Press, 1971), p. 48.

4. Francisco López de Gómara, translated and edited by Lesley Byrd Simpson, *Cortés: The Life of the Conqueror by His Secretary* (Berkeley, Calif.: University of California Press, 1966), p. 11.

5. William H. Prescott, *History of the Conquest of Mexico* (New York: Modern Library, 1998), pp. 163–164.

6. White, p. 49.

7. Johnson, p. 19.

8. White, p. 50.

9. Ibid., p. 54.

10. Thomas, p. 111.

11. White, p. 56.

12. Bernal Diaz del Castillo, *The Conquest of New Spain* (London: Penguin Books, 1963), p. 47.

13. White, pp. 58–59.

14. Prescott, p. 186.

Chapter 2. A New World Calls

1. William Weber Johnson, *Cortés* (Boston: Little, Brown & Co., 1975), p. 6.

2. Hugh Thomas, *Conquest: Montezuma, Cortés, and the Fall of Old Mexico* (New York: Simon & Schuster, 1993), p. 122.

3. Johnson, p. 8.

4. Francisco López de Gómara, translated and edited by Lesley Byrd Simpson, *Cortés: The Life of the Conqueror by His Secretary* (Berkeley, Calif.: University of California Press, 1966), p. 8.

5. Ibid.

6. Ibid.

7. Nancy Stanley and Sirena Turner, "Hernán Cortés: The Man Behind the Mystique," n.d., <http://www.cofc.edu/chrestomathy/vol3/stanley&turner.pdf> (April 17, 2007).

8. Thomas, p. 136.

9. William H. Prescott, *History of the Conquest of Mexico* (New York: Modern Library, 1998), p. 189.

10. Stanley and Turner, "Hernán Cortés: The Man Behind the Mystique."

11. Thomas, p. 146.

12. De Gómara, p. 25.

13. Prescott, p. 192.

14. De Gómara, p. 23.

15. Prescott, p. 194.

16. Bernal Díaz del Castillo, *The Conquest of New Spain* (London: Penguin Books, 1963), p. 58.

17. Richard Lee Marks, *Cortés: The Great Adventurer and the Fate of Aztec Mexico* (New York: Alfred A. Knopf, 1993), pp. 41–42.

18. Ibid., pp. 43–44.

19. Ibid., p. 44.

20. Diaz del Castillo, pp. 64–65.

21. Marks, pp. 47–48.

22. Ibid., p. 49.

23. Johnson, p. 38.

24. Diaz del Castillo, p. 75.

25. Marks, p. 51.

26. Jaime Suchlicki, *Mexico: from Montezuma to NAFTA, Chiapas, and Beyond* (Washington, D.C.: Brassey's, Inc., 1996), p. 21.

Chapter 3. A Battle of Wills: Cortés and Montezuma

1. William Weber Johnson, *Cortés* (Boston: Little, Brown & Co., 1975), pp. 42–43.

2. Francisco López de Gómara, translated and edited by Lesley Byrd Simpson, *Cortés: The Life of the Conqueror by His Secretary* (Berkeley, Calif.: University of California Press, 1966), pp. 54–55.

3. Johnson, p. 57.

4. López de Gómara, pp. 57–58.

5. "La Malinche: Harlot or Heroine?" *Mexconnect*, December 1997, <http://www.mexconnect.com/en/articles/224-la-malinche-harlot-or-heroine> (May 11, 2009).

6. Richard Lee Marks, *Cortés: The Great Adventurer and the Fate of Aztec Mexico* (New York: Alfred A. Knopf, 1993), pp. 62–63.

7. Johnson, pp. 62–63.

8. Ibid., pp. 66–67.

9. Ibid., p. 68.

10. Jon Manchip White, *Cortés and the Downfall of the Aztec Empire* (New York: St. Martin's Press, 1971), p. 189.

11. "Cortés Burns His Boats," *PBS: Conquistadores—Cortés,* n.d., <http://www.pbs.org/conquistadors/cortes/cortes_d00.html> (October 25, 2006).

12. White, p. 195.

13. Davíd Carrasco with Scott Sessions, *Daily Life of the Aztecs: People of the Sun and Earth* (Westport, Conn.: Greenwood Press, 1998), p. 66.

14. "Hernán Cortés: From Second Letter to Charles V, 1520," *Modern History Sourcebook,* n.d., <http//www.Fordham.edu/halsall/mod/1520cortes.html> (July 31, 2007).

15. White, p. 201.

16. Johnson, p. 114.

17. Bernal Díaz del Castillo, *The Conquest of New Spain* (London: Penguin Books, 1963), p. 242.

18. Johnson, pp. 116–118.

19. Carrasco and Sessions, pp. 210–211, 216.

20. Johnson, pp. 124–125.

21. López de Gómara, pp. 193–194.

Chapter 4. "Fortune Always Favors the Bold"

1. William Weber Johnson, *Cortés* (Boston: Little, Brown & Co., 1975), p. 135.

2. Ibid., pp. 137–138.

3. "Massacre in the Main Temple," *Modern History Sourcebook: Aztec Account of the Conquest of Mexico,* n.d., <http://www.fordham.edu/halsall/mod/aztecs1.html> (January 8, 2007).

4. Bernal Díaz del Castillo, *The Conquest of New Spain* (London: Penguin Books, 1963), p. 289.

5. Johnson, p. 148.

6. John Pohl and Charles M. Robinson III, *Aztecs and Conquistadores: The Spanish Invasion and the Collapse of the Aztec Empire* (Botley, Oxford, U.K.: Osprey Publishing, Ltd., 2005), pp. 137–138.

7. Francisco López de Gómara, translated and edited by Lesley Byrd Simpson, *Cortés: The Life of the Conqueror by His Secretary* (Berkeley, Calif.: University of California Press, 1966), p. 222.

8. Johnson, p. 152.

9. Richard Lee Marks, *Cortés: The Great Adventurer and the Fate of Aztec Mexico* (New York: Alfred A. Knopf, 1993), pp. 173–174.

10. López de Gómara, p. 229.

11. Marks, p. 189.

12. Ibid., p. 202.

13. Ibid., pp. 190–191.

14. Miguel Leon-Portillo, *The Broken Spears: The Aztec Account of the Conquest of Mexico* (Boston: Beacon Press, 1990), p. 93.

15. Johnson, pp. 158–159.

16. William H. Prescott, *History of the Conquest of Mexico* (New York: Modern Library, 1998), pp. 544–545.

17. Johnson, pp. 163–164.

18. Díaz del Castillo, p. 350.

19. "Two Worlds Meet," *PBS*, n.d., <http://www.pbs.org/opb/*conquistadors*/mexico/adventure3/a6.htm#txt> (October 25, 2006).

20. Jon Manchip White, *Cortés and the Downfall of the Aztec Empire* (New York: St. Martin's Press, 1971), p. 267.

21. Hernán Cortés, *Letters from Mexico* (New York: Grossman, 1971), p. 251.

22. Johnson, pp. 168–169.

23. "Our Lady of Guadalupe," n.d., <http://www.sancta.org/intro.html> (May 11, 2009).

24. Lesley Byrd Simpson, *Many Mexicos* (Berkeley, Calif.: University of California Press, 1967), p. 31.

25. Nancy Stanley and Sirena Turner, "Hernán Cortés: the Man Behind the Mystique," *Chrestomathy: Annual Review of Undergraduate Research at the College of Charleston,* 2004, <http://www.cofc.edu/chrestomathy/vol3/stanley&turner.pdf> (April 17, 2007).

26. Simpson, pp. 32–33.

Chapter 5. The Legacy of Conquest

1. Victor Alba, *The Horizon Concise History of Mexico* (New York: American Heritage Publishing Co., 1973), pp. 13–14.

2. Jaime Suchlicki, *Mexico: From Montezuma to NAFTA, Chiapas, and Beyond* (Washington, D.C.: Brassey's, 1996), pp. 20–21.

3. Serge Gruzinski, *The Aztecs: Rise and Fall of an Empire* (New York: Harry N. Abrams, Publishers, 1992), p. 22.

4. Miguel Leon-Portillo, ed., *The Broken Spears: The Aztec Account of the Conquest of Mexico* (Boston: Beacon Press, 1992), pp. xxxii–xxxiii.

5. David Carrasco with Scott Sessions, *Daily Life of the Aztecs: People of the Sun and Earth* (Westport, Conn.: Greenwood Press, 1998), pp. 56–57.

6. William H. Prescott, "Aztec Society in Transition," The Aztecs, Part Six, 1992, <http://history-world.org/aztec6.htm> (June 1, 2009).

7. Miguel Leon-Portillo, *Aztec Thought and Culture* (Norman, Okla.: University of Oklahoma Press, 1963), pp. 160–163.

8. Miguel Leon-Portillo, *The Broken Spears: The Aztec Account of the Conquest of Mexico* (Boston: Beacon Press, 1990), p. 146.

9. "Life in the American Colonies," n.d., <http://encarta.msn.com/encyclopedia_761595536_2/Spanish_Empire.html> (November 4, 2006).

10. Tim L. Merrill and Ramón Miró, eds., *Mexico: A Country Study* (Washington, D.C.: Federal Research Division, Library of Congress, 1997), pp. 10–11.

11. Ibid., p. 13.

12. "Spanish Empire: Shifting Identities," n.d., <http://encarta.msn.com/encyclopedia_761595536_2/Spanish_Empire.html> (January 21, 2008).

13. Alba, p. 55.

14. Lesley Byrd Simpson, *Many Mexicos* (Berkeley, Calif.: University of California Press, 1967), pp. 210–215.

15. "Mexican Revolution: the Revolt Begins," n.d., <http://Encarta.msn.com/encyclopedia_761588457/Mexican Revolution.html> (January 21, 2008).

16. Alba, pp. 143–144.

17. "59 Revolutions Image Info," August 2005, <http://placeholdermedia.com/projects/59revolutions/assets/images/Zapatista.jpg> (May 12, 2009).

18. Merrill and Miró, pp. xlii–xliii.

19. Philip L. Russell, *The Chiapas Rebellion* (Austin, Tex.: Mexico Resource Center, 1995), p. 45.

Chapter 6. A Dark and Tangled History

1. Tony Cohan, *On Mexican Time: A New Life in San Miguel* (New York: Broadway Books, 2000), p. 233.

2. T. Walter Wallbank and Arnold Schrier, *Living World History* (Glenview, Ill.: Scott, Foresman, 1974), p. 341–342.

3. Ibid., p. 264.

4. Ibid., p. 521.

5. Ibid., p. 522.

6. Joseph A. Ellis, *Latin America: Its Peoples and Institutions* (Encino, Calif.: Glencoe Publishing, 1975), pp. 142–144.

7. "Key Moments in the Hispanic History of South America," *Celebrate Hispanic Heritage,* n.d., <http://teacher.scholastic.com/activities/Hispanic/sahistory.htm> (May 11, 2008).

8. "Latin America," *The World Book Encyclopedia* (Chicago: World Book, Inc., 2005), p. 108.

9. "Antonio López de Santa Anna," *New Perspectives on the West,* n.d., <http://www.pbs.org/weta/thewest/people/s_z/santaanna.htm> (May 11, 2009).

10. Alma Guillermoprieto, *Looking for History: Dispatches from Latin America* (New York: Pantheon Books, 2001), p. 194.

11. John Charles Chasteen, *Born in Blood and Fire: A Concise History of Latin America* (New York: W. W. Norton & Company, 2001), p. 25.

12. E. Bradford Burns, *Latin America: A Concise Interpretive History* (Englewood Cliffs, N.J.: Prentice-Hall, Inc., 1972), p. 164.

13. Susana Cano, Juan Sandoval, and Norma Torres, "La Malinche Remains Controversial," n.d., <http://www.epcc.edu/nwlibrary/borderlands/17_la_Malinche.htm> (April 26, 2008).

14. Erasmo Perez, "Travel Report," Cortés Pass (Mexico State), March 5, 2006, <http://erasmoperez.blogspot.com/2007/03/paso-de-cortes-mexico-state-050306_16.html> (April 7, 2008).

15. Peter Rashkin, Herschel Sarnoff, and Da na Bagdasarian, "Cortés and Malinche," *The Conquest of Mexico,* 2005, <http://thedagger.com/archive/conquest/Malinche.html> (April 7, 2008).

16. Cano, Sandoval, and Torres, "La Malinche Remains Controversial."

Glossary

brigantine—A large, two-masted sailing ship.

cacíque—A tribal chieftain who ran the tribe's affairs and led its warriors into battle.

campesíno—A peasant farmer, whether Indian or *mestizo,* who often is forced to work his fields with outdated tools and equipment.

caudíllo—A Latin American dictator who gains and holds power by force of arms and personality.

chínampas—The artificial islands that the Aztecs used for growing food on the lake that surrounded the city of Tenochtitlán.

conquístadores—Literally, "conquerors." The term describes the Spanish soldiers who conquered the Indians of the New World.

críollo—A Latin American born in the New World to Spanish parents.

ejído—Communal land set aside by law for the use of Indian and mestizo farmers.

encomíenda—A land grant that gave Spanish settlers the right to demand tribute and free labor from the local Indians. In return, the *encomenderos* (land-owners) were expected to protect and Christianize their workers.

"flowery wars"—Wars fought by the Aztecs for the purpose of taking prisoners who would be sacrificed to their gods.

gachupíne—An upper-class Latin American who was born in Spain to Spanish parents. The *gachupines* thought of themselves as superior to the more numerous *criollos* and *mestizos.*

Huitzilopochtli—The Aztecs believed that this fearsome war god had a voracious appetite for human sacrifice.

Latin America—The vast geographic region that stretches from Mexico southward to the tip of South America, including the islands of the West Indies.

mestizo—A Latin American of mixed race, the child of a Spaniard and an Indian.

Nahuatl—The written and spoken language of the Aztecs.

Quetzalcoatl—The Aztec creation god, sometimes known as "the plumed serpent." Prophecies said that the light-skinned, bearded god would return in a One Reed year—and Cortés arrived in such a year.

repartimiento—A land grant program that replaced the *encomienda*. The *repartimiento* limited the number of workdays a year a landowner could demand from the local Indians. Despite the new limits, many owners still abused their Indian workers.

Further Reading

BOOKS

Bingham, Jane. *The Aztec Empire*. Chicago: Raintree, 2007.

Burgan, Michael. *The Spanish Conquest of America*. New York: Chelsea House, 2007.

Calvert, Patricia. *Hernando Cortés: Fortune Favored the Bold*. New York: Benchmark Books, 2003.

Lourie, Peter. *Hidden World of the Aztec*. Honesdale, Pa.: Boyds Mill Press, 2006.

Ramen, Fred. *Hernán Cortés: The Conquest of Mexico and the Aztec Empire*. New York: Rosen Pub. Group, 2004.

Stein, R. Conrad. *The Story of Mexico: Cortés and the Spanish Conquest*. Greensboro, N.C.: Morgan Reynolds Pub., 2007.

INTERNET ADDRESSES

The Aztec Empire
<http://www.latinamericanstudies.org/aztecs.htm>

Conquistadors: The Fall of the Aztecs
<http://www.pbs.org/conquistadors/cortes/cortes_a00.html>

Modern History Sourcebook. Hernán Cortés: From Second Letter to Charles V, 1520
<http://www.fordham.edu/halsall/mod/1520cortes.html>

Index